BALE FIRE

Born in 1963 in Johnstone, Jim Carruth grew up on his family's farm near Kilbarchan. His first collection *Bovine Pastoral* came out in 2004 and in 2009 he was awarded a Robert Louis Stevenson Fellowship. He has published multiple collections and chapbooks attracting both praise and awards, including the McLellan Poetry Prize and the Callum Macdonald Memorial Award. His verse novella *Killochries*, originally published in 2015, was shortlisted for the Saltire Society Scottish Poetry Book of the Year, the Seamus Heaney Centre for Poetry Prize and the Fenton Aldeburgh Prize for first collection. *Bale Fire* is the follow up to *Black Cart* (2017). Jim is the current poet laureate of Glasgow.

BALE FIRE

Jim Carruth

First published in Great Britain in 2019 by
Polygon, an imprint of Birlinn Ltd.

Birlinn Ltd
West Newington House
10 Newington Road
Edinburgh EH9 1QS

www.polygonbooks.co.uk

ISBN 978 1 84697 500 4

British Library Cataloguing-in-Publication Data
A catalogue record for this book is available on
request from the British Library.

The publisher gratefully acknowledges investment from
Creative Scotland towards the publication of this book.

Typeset in Verdigris MVB by Polygon, Edinburgh
Printed and bound by Bell & Bain, Ltd, Glasgow

For Lorna, David, Hannah and Paul

CONTENTS

II. HOME

III. FORGOTTEN FURROWS & FIELD SONGS

AUTHOR'S NOTE

Each of the footers in this collection are taken from aspects of rural life. The footers in the first section, Change in the Weather, are common agricultural diseases, giving a sense of an ailing community in need of healing. In the second section, Home, I have named each page after the surnames of local farming families, bringing together the local and mythical. And in the final section, the footers signify the endevours of harvest, linking the products with the human cost of their production.

'On the Turn' (p. 17): In July 2019 a national rural crime network report highlighted that rural victims of abuse were half as likely to report it than average, and were likely to experience abuse for 25% longer with rural isolation often used as a weapon.

'Trouble at the Farm' (p. 19): One farmer a week takes their own life in the UK.

balefire: n. bonfire, beacon fire, funeral pyre

as if one day we simply became lower case,
language discarded, ridiculed, titles removed,
deeds surrendered, paragraphs dismantled;
without a willing translator from the outside,
our speech turned to a babbling of streams,
shrinking to less than a sentence or phrase,
little more than a cluster of words fenced in,
forgotten, the withering of our written word
a blighted crop dying on the page's landscape.
is there a single linguist left to irrigate our hill
from this almost empty well or an alchemist
who could gather in the final breaths of place,
guttural vowels, the grunted clods of consonants
and create from these brief fragments of sound
an echo louder than its diminished source?

CHANGE IN THE WEATHER

A community is the mental and spiritual condition of knowing that the place is shared, and that the people who share the place define and limit the possibilities of each other's lives. It is the knowledge that people have of each other, their concern for each other, their trust in each other, the freedom with which they come and go among themselves.

Wendell Berry

Because the Land are We

Because the land
are we:

the days,
a gift of breath;

the weeks,
muscle-burden, sweat;

the months,
skin wearing the soil;

the years,
hands taking the furrows;

our lifetime,
a body harvest-borne;

our death,
bones to the earth;

each new voice repeats
the ancient song,

*Because the land
are we.*

Birth

Having allowed the young heifer her turn,
a fruitless afternoon in the calving pen
that did nothing but drain her of energy,
I return to her after the milking of the others,
place my hand on her back; talk calmly,
loop my bale strings over the soft hooves
of front legs barely showing under her tail
and wrap the other end of the frayed twine
around my waist, ready to save two lives.
When she rests I will too; when she pushes
I will lean back and add weight to each move.
The progress we make, working together,
is measured in the length of legs that inch out.
You can't rush or the mother will suffer more.
In the growing pauses she takes to recover
my mind is filled with other births, life's thread,
each new born holding on to find the light –
our children were sliced free from a womb,
saved through the help of essential hands.
Now the nose and the strong head appears:
sticky, the large tongue too, hanging loose,
a job still not done, a set of wide shoulders
and little room. I tilt them slightly to and fro
till the calf is released to drop by its mother.
The speed of this at the end always a surprise.
I untie its legs, stand back a bit and watch.
She turns to her own calf, starts to lick her.
I find wonder every time in this moment,
just the one parent and child. I, who was born
while my father finished milking his cows.

Leabaidh na Ba Baine
the bed of the white cow

The giant Fingal cared so much
for his favourite white heifer,

he used his huge hands as shovels,
scooped a hollow out of the hill,

sculpted an earthen mould
to cup her coarse-haired flanks,

shaped its sides with furrows
that echoed every rib of her frame:

a loving support to keep her safe,
to hold her during the hours of labour

as if she was offering up her calf
into the cradle of his palms.

School Milk

It should have rescued me from the rigid desk,
my clumsy writing constrained between narrow lines,
my numbers following the strict rules of the abacus,
the strap-backed warnings to *keep off the grass*.

First disappointment was the alien pyramid:
waxed cardboard sides a straw would not puncture,
to the amusement of my fellow pupils,
Farmer's son can't even drink his milk.

But worse by far was the taste –
not the frothy thick cream, but lifeless, cold.
Maybe it was the limitations of the straw,
or the two-mile journey that pricked its bubbles,

or it came from a different herd, another district,
lines of sad cows shut up inside all year,
chained in cubicles, kept from the grass,
missing the fields, dying for the bell.

The Trade

Son, today when I stare at my cupped hands
I remember how as a calf she suckled my fingers;

that sticky tickle of her rough tongue,
how she would follow me around the pen.

Later as a heifer, the energy in her leap and bound
as she came to my first call.

Then motherhood, my hand on her warm flank,
her milk filling pails for both of our children.

When I look into my hands, Jack, I see more
magic in memory than I'll ever get from these beans.

Ars, Artis

i. An Introduction to Docking and Castration

He tells me
his great grandfather
would have used his teeth

to pull off their testicles.
But that was then;
this is now.

He takes in one hand
a bleating male lamb,
twelve days old,

while his other
wields a sharp blade
with slotted grip.

He pulls back
the youngster's new skin,
hacks the tail away,

slices the scrotum
in a single arc,
withdraws the stones

all in a minute and a half.
This practical art
has finality and grace.

ii. Ploughing is Performance

Violence is in the art.
Coulter blade breaks ground,

slices through to the dance,
the strip of tired sod
lifted up by the share,

rolled over by the mouldboard,
        left on its back,
in the wake of the plough;

burying that strangled mat,
weeds, last season's grass,
raising up folds of new colour,

breaking the grip of the tight fist,
releasing the ridged fingers –
        soft collapse,
                sigh of soil.

In a single furrow laid down
the finished pattern of field.

A Village Elder's Advice on the White Crow

Why do you search
for false auguries of hope?

Nothing followed the triple rainbow,
or last winter's one wild rose.

Now this feathered messiah.
Can I speak plainly here:

a white crow is still a crow;
a lifeless sheep is still a corpse;

a bloated corpse is still a meal
for your white crow. It

still rises with its flock,
flies with its flock,

still falls with the black
on the weak and the dead.

A Killing

The photograph in the paper is of mourners –
the two sisters pristine in school uniform.
A favourite pet shot, one of the family.
The spectre of the villain farmer is drawn
in clumsy broad strokes of black and white.
The page where the story ends does not frame
the scene witnessed in colour by the shepherd –
the brown mongrel panting in the new grass,
dew drops sparkling its halo in early light.
A wreath of red around the hound's mouth;
around its body, dead lambs spread like petals.

Musk

Less than a week after first cut
the fields are covered in shit;
slurry spread thick in arcs,
a dark fan laid down on the land,
a giant paw-print, tacky and rank.

Something of the beast prowls
untamed through the village,
hangs the air in clammy heat,
holds us close, its breath foul
as all our sins come to visit.

Even behind closed doors
it will not leave us;
we are stained by its scent.
Its body brooding, becoming crust,
drying on the earth like a mask.

Witness

A voice was heard in Ramah – Jeremiah

and her voice
      through the wall
was like something
often heard
      at hay-time

when leverets
      lie up
in the long grass
invisible
      to the mower

motionless
      pretending
they're not there
crouched
      as if in prayer
to remain untouched

but found
      by feckless men:

their final cries
like blades
      through skin.

Ratman

This was the nickname that stuck,
though the rat he trapped in a sack at harvest time,
as a pet, survived only for another six months.
He kept it half-starved in a cage on the shelf

where it could watch him chewing his meals
of caught, shot or cheap cuts, sucking goodness
out of the marrow of an old hock for hours.
He boasted that he fed it only when it cried out,

the way the schoolgirls had done in the village,
when he spooked them with his stare, his odd manner,
his warnings on how he'd make them whistle his tune;
how virginity was a milk tooth overdue for pulling.

Sharp-tongued women now, they're quick to point out
that the rat was most likely his only real companion
on those nights together, both gnawing at thrown scraps,
a long winter gnawing on them.

On the Turn

Marrying without her father's consent was theft.
So I went just once, after their leaving,
to that run-down smallholding they had found:
some windowless shack with a roof of tin.
By then he only had four Friesians breathing,
he'd try to milk on his few sober days,
as she worked miracles from the poor ground.
When I got there she would not let me in.
Crying infants clung to her, and she turned
away to hide the bruises on her face.
And do you know what that drunk muttered
from behind the bolted door as I left?
Don't forget boy, to get the golden butter
everyone knows you have to rock the churn.

The Wife's Tale

He is still out there working the dark,
checking his mothers, lantern swinging
through the hill fields like a firefly,
his meal long-cold,
                    the children in bed.
I wait for this man who's dour as hell,
buffeted by the first autumn storm,
more stubborn than his beasts.

Trouble at the Farm

Black smoke billows down the valley.
I leave the harvest, set off on foot.

Others join as I head through
the cacophony of frightened beasts.

Those that can, take flight;
the rest stampede.

The dark cloud takes the sun
and more than this day is lost.

The old tractor is a charred hull
at the centre of a wheat field aflame.

Two dead collies and a shotgun:
a twisted triangle in the yard.

All the windows are broken,
the children crying inside.

The mother is screaming at us,
Please don't go into the barn.

But I do go into the barn.
And now that trouble lives in me.

The Farmer Doesn't Want a Wife

The famer doesn't want a wife.
She wants a better March than last year,
without the worst of the snows and storms
that ravaged her Blackface flock.

She wants more energy for this season –
let there be fewer dead lambs, more twins.
She wants the cost of feed to fall,
next Autumn's market prices to rise.

She wants both her misfiring quad bike
and her young collie to be more reliable.
She wants the absent, foreign landlord
to keep the rent the same a little longer.

She wants the support of neighbours
when there is work needing many hands
but not when they offer advice at length,
teaching her granny to suck eggs as they do.

She wants time to fix the barn roof,
sort two fences and a hundred other tasks.
Also, she would really love a newer tractor
but that'll have to wait for another year.

The farmer doesn't want a wife.
She wants early morning starts to be later
and still achieve all that's needing done
before watching the sun set on the hill.

Orf

The Other Wilson

for Gerrie

The Other Wilson was different
everyone said so, and often.
He wasn't like the rest.

Neighbours brought him baskets of pleasantries,
concern with its crusts cut off,
to glean new evidence on his hovel –
that smallest of smallholdings.

His roof's a disgrace;
slates litter the steading.

It was said that his cattle were so thin
they lent against each other to cough;
a herd of hoarse barks echoed down the valley.

His children: barefoot, flea-bitten,
un-schooled, and their language is choice.

The Other Wilson gathered his own harvest of
unpaid bills, debts, summons, visits:
animal welfare, factor, banker, social workers
all came and went.

And everywhere that smell.
No wonder she left.

Words, relentless as west-coast rain,
threatened to wash him away,
though he clung on year after year.

His poor mother.
God rest her soul.

The Other Wilson was the one
to make us feel better about ourselves,
so his midnight flit without warning
winded us like a low blow,

left us speechless, bereft in a way
the loss of a close relative could never do.
We needed him, we needed The Other Wilson
to stay with us and fail.

Little Black Hen

It was never about the little black hen,
no matter how much she was talked of
with such sadness within the family.

Even the youngest child could recount,
through tears, the tale of good and evil –
one more martyr to this long conflict

between generations of neighbours.
Portrayed now as a close personal friend,
she was never given that status in life.

For this frankly anonymous sickly fowl,
now heavily feathered with elegy,
pecked the yard with the rest of her kind.

Nothing worth noting – an average layer.
Her eggs were neither many nor large,
her yolk was not some special yellow,

though, on her death, all this changed.
It was never about the little black hen,
but the pot they said she ended up in.

Beyond the Headlands

Beyond the farm's last headland,
the furthest furrow in the parish,
everything changes, if you let it.
Tall blackthorn guards a darkness
for those who risk the journey
and step into that ancient lane,
the other side of the barred gate.

The village elders, who remember
rumour and gossip as teaching,
call that walk the falling away.
The few who return are altered,
with a strange new coarseness
in gait and manner, joyless,
slow to share their many demons.
Their tales are rambling, incoherent,
holding little common ground
for those who stayed behind.

They cannot remember the days
of the festivals, will not sing
the old songs, nor help with harvest.
At night though huddled closest
to the home hearth they feel a chill.
To look into their empty stares
is to find the hurt of a double grief,
to be lost and found and lost again.

Bale String

An ageing bale string reined in too often
over the long distance begins to fray.

At your city desk, emptied out to a shadow,
a doe's hung carcass drained for a week.

Faith in the physical and real dismantled,
you call home to a phone unanswered.

You strain to see in a fading negative
a photograph of fields once in colour;

to follow the pale outline of memory,
unravelling fictions of another life.

When muck and dirt are the stain of Cain
you never want to be removed,

a bale string snapped now will leave you
holding one end, unable to ever get back.

Transferable Skills

This interview of grey suits is not going well.
They have already mentioned those three words,
letting me go, as though I was being released

back into the wild like all those animals
I used to catch in jam jars as a child,
crested newts, warty toads kept for a week

then dropped outside in the long grass
when novelty and interest waned,
that regular chore of caring too much.

Next they talk of competencies and fit,
these uncivil servants in their air-conditioned pods.
Do they really get dealing with uncertainty,

how to cope with the vagaries of the seasons,
a late fall of snow that covers the hill during lambing.
Could they manage a budget with the income so low,

or work through the night with a difficult calving?
I can listen for the mother's bellow and know
what must be done to save them both.

I, who understand and take responsibility
for every life that breathes upon the farm,
am deemed to lack the necessary skills.

I, who can pick up the scent of a dead tup
in a ditch, half a mile downwind,
and recognise it for what it is and was.

I, who can smell the stench of something now.

HOME

Glorious Odysseus, what you are after is a sweet homecoming
Odyssey, Book XI

i. The Journey of Telemachus

This is not about a separation
marked by mountains and seas
or a distance to be blamed
on the whims of petulant gods.
Memories are never enough
to defend the threats to home.
You must rise before first light,
spend those waking days with him,
begin to understand more fully
that the same complex love that calls
hungry children in from the fields
orders an old collie to stay behind.

ii. Suitors

The shepherd's prize ewe,
heavy-bellied, cowped and helpless. Crows
gather around her like suitors.

With the shepherd elsewhere
this cowardice falling over itself, eager
for easy pickings of warm flesh.

They parade on her trembling frame,
an arrogant strut of the victors,
impatient for the banquet to come.

iii. Leaving the Field

Leaving the field
hunched, shuffling, fatigued,
facing up daily
to advancing fronts,
struggling to lift one foot
in front of the other;

foot-rot hobble,
pneumonia coughing,

shitting blood, lame
and blind in a quarter.

iv. Setting Out

I am in command
of the vessels,

patrolling the lower deck,
my bovine crew each side,

a pulsing drumbeat
setting out their effort.

Pulling together,
we sense the swell,

edge out of the harbour
on a high tide of milk.

v. Cyclops – the Shepherd

Easy to mock his singular focus,
a herdsman dedicated to the flock,
to mimic his rustic strength.

Happy to take his milk and meat,
cling to the thickness of wool,
without taking time to look closer

at his constant watch on the hill;
how he nurtures every lamb and will
sacrifice his life for them.

vi. Sower

An art, the way he scatters the future,
mastering a steady pace, a wide arc,
a swinging throw far and even.

From the pouch around his waist
he broadcasts a field of seeds
on a breeze of his own making.

An eager novice keen to impress,
the seed I fling falls short in clumps,
shipwrecked, at once becalmed.

vii. Piggery

Hers was the only piggery on the hill;
left to run it when her father died.
Her looks, her blond hair, her estate

drew many farmers' sons up the track,
unperturbed by the smell of the place,
eager to have their snouts in her trough.

Young lads entranced by her singing
didn't notice at first the pigs in the pen.
Eventually they sensed something wrong,

their appearance unnatural – a type of hybrid
seen sometimes when breed jumps breed
or that look you get when cousins marry.

viii. Metamorphosis

Back of the byre
round bales in bin bags

piled high like a dark slice
of honeycomb,

each cylinder
tied with string, airtight,

their wild mare's ragged tails
flapping in the gale.

One piece tears itself free,
a wind-blown raven in flight.

ix. The Fall of Elpenor

He'd lived alone the decade since she left
so nobody heard the slip, the scream,
the heavy thud, the crack of his neck.

His body lay there outside the old shed,
crumpled like a swallow fledgling
fallen from sanctuary's cupped nest,
dropped inches from the ladder
that should've been his safe passage.

The neighbour who found him
smelt the cheap blend on his lips
though his breathing had ceased.
It was not the whisky that killed him.
It was the years through which he fell.

x. Field of the Dead

Leave him alone:
there is no madness here,
no rush now.
What you have to do
can wait.

Give him this time
to spend
in this place.
It's what he is owed
for the suffering.

He is talking
to his lost brothers.
He is dancing
with his sisters.

Leave him
in this field
of ghosts.
Only here,
he is not alone.

xi. Neighbours on the Hill

It is always a story of trial and effort . . .

Tantalos,
reaping the sparsest of harvests,
as each summer, local springs shrink away.

Sisyphus,
straining to remove from his field the rocks
that return year after year.

Tityos,
a broken man working those difficult acres,
cursing the crows who will not let him be.

. . . never a story of the journey complete.

Herakles,
toiling with the shackles of the hill
till it took his sanity, his family.

xii. Song of the Siren

Old men, what first beached you on this hill,
stopped short your wandering years,
anchored you for generations to this land?

No mavis or blackbird has that kind of hold;
no whistled tune from wind-blown spruce;
you are not swayed by the pull of the moon.

The ancient ley lines are not your jailor,
nor are you trapped by threats in distant hills,
hemmed in by the superstitions of the dead.

Old men, it is the earth that sings to you.
Her song, that binds your hands to this place,
outlasts your final breath, buries you below.

xiii. Cailleach (Skyla)

She rarely left her hovel cut into the hill,
that thatched dampness attracting the dark,
but spent all of her remaining days
watching seasons change at a window.

She'd gaze on the high pool of Charybdis
where the brave and foolish children
would swim in the short summer,
despite the stories, the finds of bones.

They ignored her soft persistent calling
to come inside for juice and scones.
Heeding the warnings of their parents,
they teased her with hurtful rhymes sung

from the safety of the deep waters,
where years ago, on a day just like this,
a strong current had grasped a boy's
legs and dragged him down.

xiv. Hill of Silence

There was of course that other hill to the south:
a hill of green fields, enough grass for all seasons,

seven flocks of sheep with the finest fleece,
seven herds of cattle fit and firm of foot.

Their chosen guardians grew complacent,
confident in their breeding lines and future.

Unwanted guests moved among them,
animals were taken, sacrificed on the pyre

by outsiders desperate to quench a hunger,
but ill-prepared for the anger of the gods.

xv. Storm

After all that had been
blighted by the barren and sick,

everyone agreed he was due
the return of a good harvest-year.

What he got instead, high on the hill,
was the brunt of the winter storm.

When the byre roof came down
on his sleeping beasts and all were lost

it was not hard to believe
in a god of harsh judgements.

xvi. Argos

What is left for the working dog,
when the master calls no more?

No need to go away back,
to be sent out beyond the flock,

busy days of fetch and drive,
working the hill to whistle and shout

from lamb to thrawn ram,
to bring each sheep back home,

to let the master hear your bark
and know that you are near.

Those days are lost like sheep,
buried deep in winter's drifts.

Patient, they wait for the shepherd,
his long stick pushing through snow,

to find them breathing still,
dig them out, to run on the hill again.

What is left for the working dog,
when the master calls no more?

xvii. The Night of Fox

Under the wire he came,
years after they'd forgotten
his strength and threat,

the merest scent of him
no longer roosting
in their shared memory.

They dropped their guard
to a red dervish
lunging at their necks;

peck of bantam beak,
splay-toed claws and spur
no match for the violence

of jaw snap and flesh tear,
clucked frenzy, screaming fowl
locked in manic clutches.

The flock slaughtered,
lost in a feathered blizzard,
blood rupturing the hutch.

xviii. What Happened to the Crows

They took what was not theirs,
defiled the master's field,
plucked the heart from his harvest.

So after the feast he had them dance
in one line swaying in the wind,
their necks noosed, hanging from a fence.

xix. Embrace

Father was it always about this moment:
our distances replaced by a closeness, not

a reaching out three times
for the empty embrace of mother's ghost;

an offer made at the journey's end,
returning to reclaim what's lost?

In this wordless moment on the hill,
acceptance and forgiveness bud

a revelation in an unaccustomed holding
of hereditary flesh and bone.

xx. Homecoming

Never lose this hunger for home.
At the end of the day
after long labour in the fields,
backache and setting sun,
you descend the hill again,
soul-tired with heavy steps,
a weariness that buckles legs
from honest hours. Knowing
you could have done no more,
you watch for a kindling of lights,
for smoke rising from the first fires;
at your feet, collies swim the dusk.
After all this time you could find
your way back blind.

FORGOTTEN FURROWS
& FIELD SONGS

*Quand on est dans la merde jusqu'au cou, il ne reste
plus qu'à chanter.*

Samuel Beckett

The Songs of George Brann

Run, birds, run,
The master's coming with a gun,
You must fly and I must run,
Away birds away.

From the age of nine, for pennies,
George Brann shouted for a living,
the last of the bird scarers,
patrolling acres of Kentish corn.

Though he loved birdsong, the most
sought-after hollerer
        south of the Thames
walked his days drowning it out

blowing a penny whistle,
swinging a wooden clapper,
rattling pebbles in a tin,
yelling and yodelling charms.

Seven decades left him deaf
to the notes of nightingale and thrush.
Canute lost in his shrinking kingdom,
each day he'd scream till hoarse.

Run, birds, run,
The master's coming with a gun,
You must fly and I must run,
Away birds away.

Calypso

When the sun at last turns up the heat,
and old streams shrink to trickled flow,

a chorus rises in the evergreens,
as on the hill the dry winds blow.

When the yellow sway of oilseed
is harvest dancing for the show,

into the face of those southerlies,
you will hear me sing calypso.

Der Ring des Nibelungen

Sixteen hours
in the field

to complete
the harvest cycle:

ploughshare
to reaping blade,

dry days
are our gold,

ripe barley
our song sung loud,

black clouds
approaching like gods

could wreck all
our bale towers.

Only Human

I stopped my walk, climbed the gate
to help an old farmer, cursing his deaf god,
to bring in the last of a damp harvest.
He must have been struggling all day,
alone to fill that small trailer.

I cannot make more of this than it was.
I was no passing Samaritan, saving him
minutes at most, nor a reluctant volunteer,
some Simon of Cyrene shouldering
the penance of a stranger's sodden bale.

As for him, this ageing hunch-backed man,
he could not raise his head to say thanks,
nor straighten his spine to walk like a saint,
nor even resurrect the past fortnight of rain,
into one unblemished day of risen sun.

After the Corncrakes

After they'd gone, our fathers talked with sadness
of listening to their rough ratchet at harvest,
hidden from view then later silenced.

As we in turn remember our fathers' voices
calling to us as children across the same cut fields
but no longer and nowhere to be found.

The Gift

Our neighbour from Ulster – a hound for the hard work,
an eye for the quick money, the angle in a rumour,
and for sure a masters degree in gallows humour –
last week found a young beast dead from a tumour,
so he carted it to the village, his prize-winning stirk,
dropped off his harvest thanksgiving gift for the kirk.

The Song of the Oxen

To work with the oxen,
to have the oxen work for you,
you must master their song.

Learn one from the Welsh bards:
their three-line verses set well
the pace for a team in harness.

To sing the song of the oxen
is to speak to them as equals,
win them over to the yoke.

Make the song your own:
few will struggle onward for
the nightingale's flyaway notes.

To labour through heavy loam,
oxen need a deeper grounding,
sung from a guttural tongue.

To sing the song of the oxen,
your throat must be the goad,
a metronome true and steady.

To silence your voice just once
will stop the team dead, leave them
standing by a half-finished furrow.

Camshauchelt Furr

A turnt doun the auld king's caa tae fecht michtie Troy;
telt thaim a was peerie-heedit, turnt back tae ma ain glebe.
Sleekit Palamedes askit me tae pruive ma feign't plicht.

Sae a spread saut as seed, forby a chose yon donsie perr,
an ill-yokit cuddie and owse, tae badly pleuch ma grun –
furrows aw tapsalteerie as oany wind-blawn gowstie sea.

He testit me ance mair, placed ma bairn afore the beasts,
sae a pullt back hard oan the reins tae sklent awa frae him.
Wae's me, a kent this act alane wad mak me richt for war.

Christmas Baling

That wet year after war took his son,
the straw lay cut in the field for months,
a testament in rows to a harvest failed.

On Christmas morning, the land frozen,
he set to remove this public haunting:
hitched up the baler in the open shed

and was soon parading back and forth.
The old machine, shaking off its frost,
spat out dank bales as unwanted presents.

Working this day, a gift to himself,
lifting the weight of loss from the ground,
clearing the way for the plough's promise.

Clearing the Field

Our ploughing uncovers the rocks,
scattered like angry words,
wilful and defiant.

So we follow the trailer in gangs,
all day lifting and carrying,
removing their protest from the field.

Each spring a new uprising
speckles this earth, thwarts our purpose
to tame this land for harvest.

We cling to our beloved soil
though it thins through each bitter season
and the rocks shatter our blades.

Reincarnation

Half a generation ago
the ruined croft
at the back of the hill

was swearing and song,
the open arms of hospitality,
willing hands at harvest.

Today the saying out loud
of their family name
brings back faces, times.

We are here to remove
the last of the stone, rebuild
a dyke to pen the flock.

We work in silent respect,
trying to convince ourselves
it's what they would have wanted.

Logs

i.m. Alexander Hutchison (1943–2015)
In his presence, hours flew by

Long a widow, she'd collect to keep her warm:
broken branches, casualties of the storm.
Refusing all our help, she'd drag them back,
sawing each one herself, then build the stack
in the small shed, their ends sticking out white
like the accordion buttons she'd play on at night
for the neighbours who'd come to clap along
as she wrestled the dervish of breathing and song.
Wearing out young fiddlers she'd never tire.
In the small hours she was our warmth and fire.
We could tell the length of the winter ahead
from the height of the logs inside her shed.
That year the pile reached her waist, no higher,
she quipped, *Plenty here for both me and my pyre.*

Timber

Vision

He could see
the promise in a heifer,
poison in an udder's hard quarter,
pneumonia in a calf shiver,
early abortion in a ewe tremor.

He could see
hare-stew in paw-prints in the snow,
slow death in the oak's soft bark,
the fledgling in a sparrow's speckled egg,
late harvest in the first shoots.

He could see
danger in a bull's stare and stamp,
the first-prize rosette in a judge's nod,
foot-rot in the cob's hobble,
a small grave in his collie's walk.

He could see
debt in the depth of milk in the tank,
departure in his son's scowl,
the clutch of seasons left for him
hunched in the mirror's reply.

Speaking in Tongues

In the middle of the day I walk in on him, cross-legged
in the language of his kitchen.

Hieroglyphic straw litters the stone floor
where he sits in his soiled nightshirt, shroud skin.

Grey stubbled, mouth a twisted wire,
his eyes: hoofprints of dirty water,

his left arm: dead, like the end of a bale string
hangs frayed and limp by his side.

Lost, this barefoot mumbler, catatonic chanter
struggles, as I do, to find the right words.

'Brambles'

i.m. Margaret Stewart

For you the word 'brambles' symbolised patience:
waiting for green knots to ripen into soft, red fruit.
It also conjured up verge, hedgerow and scent,
September sun on your bent back; dropping berries
into baskets, small hands helping, stained fingers
and tongues, long afternoons and laughter.

This word became a crowded farm kitchen –
flour, sugar, salt rubbed together for crumble
over berries, warm stove and juices rising
then sweet pie cooling in the heart of the table
and you surrounded by family. This word,
one winter's day, was the last you ever spoke.

Bereavement Counselling from
Murdoch of Blackbyres

Listen, back in '74
I shot a crow with such force
its body cannoned into its partner,
dropped the pair from the sky.
The living shared the fall
and hard landing
of one too close.

If that winded bird
had not shaken the dust off itself,
escaped from the corpse's shackle,
raised its torn wings,
lifted itself into painful flight,
I'd have finished it off as well –
coupled them in death.

Peat

Warming my hands on this fire
that I did not work for,

I squint through the smoke
to the summer before;

watching your silhouette on the moor,
as I passed on the high road,

lifting the flaughter
to break through a matted top layer.

The following days were twisting the tusker,
slicing the peats free from the bank.

Then over the weeks to come
turning and drying of each turf,

this communal and social act
now carried out alone.

Until that final stack,
standing like a memorial

to a loved, but long-lost chieftain
whose memory flares brightly

on winter nights, like this one,
and then is lost forever.

You tell me this is not irreplaceable
but is the slowest kind of healing.

Dry Stane Dyke

for fechts awplace

In the end
it teuk twa weemen

oan ilka side o the divide
ane lang efternuin o sair graft

tae dismantle that dyke,
cairt awa aw the stanes.

Thair men-fowk lost fir oors,
fou at the hairst fair,

were inbred wi conflict
ahent the laund,

a dreich inheritance
drookit in bluid.

Anely passers-by
witnessed that day

yon weemen liltin
in a new licht,

a waulkin sang
frae common grund.

In the beginning
it teuk twa weemen.

Field Song

I dreamt Alan Lomax turned up at the farm, set up his recording equipment,
and asked for a song and all we had was a ballad handed down to Uncle Bill
who learned it off a field-hand one long Summer, who in turn had taken it
from a tinker's lass he courted, she had heard it on her granny's knee
and the trail reached further back, each song bearer bringing a bit
of themselves to the song before passing it on and passing on.
Some say it was once a lively jig about a local woman jilted –
love gone wrong – thirty verses long sparking in Scots
but now it'd become a simple slow fiddle tune;
all of its words leached out in the rain but
it was what we had left to share so
as he sat poised on a bale
we readied our bows
trusting he'd save
every last
note.

Legacy
for Les

One of these days you're gonna rise up singing.

The banker saw no worth in words,
so turned down flat, that day,
the offer of a farmer's song
as collateral for a loan for seed.

At night the farmer returned home,
buried his lyrics across furrows
set never to receive the barley.
By the morning he was gone.

Come the spring in that field,
beyond his boarded-up house,
every small word had sprouted
with such scent and promise,

it brought songbirds flocking,
eager to seek each fertile fragment,
working the lines day and night,
piecing together his forgotten tune,

until the morning they sang as one
that lost farmer's final crop.
His harvest was their chorus.
They feasted on his song.

Because the land are we (reprise)

Because the land
are we:

the days,
a gift of breath;

the weeks,
muscle-burden, sweat;

the months,
skin wearing the soil;

the years,
hands taking the furrows;

our lifetime,
a body harvest-borne;

our death,
bones to the earth;

each new voice repeats
the ancient song,

*Because the land
are we.*

ACKNOWLEDGEMENTS

I would like to thank everyone who helped shape this collection, including Gerry Cambridge, Gerrie Fellows, Vicki Husband and Sam Tongue.

I would also like to thank the editors of the following publications, where versions of some of the poems first appeared: the anthologies, *Entanglements: New Ecopoetry*; *New Writing Scotland* (28,30,31) and magazines, *Poetry Café*, *Quadrant*.

'Dry Stane Dyke' was the runner up in the McCash Poetry competition in 2013. An earlier fragment of 'Home' was the winner of the McLellan Poetry Prize 2013.